Birthdays Around the World

by Marilyn Greco

PEARSON

Scott
Foresman

Editorial Offices: Glenview, Illinois • Parsippany, New Jersey • New York, New York
Sales Offices: Needham, Massachusetts • Duluth, Georgia • Glenview, Illinois
Coppell, Texas • Ontario, California • Mesa, Arizona

Opener: DK Images; 1 (C, Bkgd) Getty Images; 3 (Bkgd) Getty Images, (C) DK Images; 4 DK Images; 5 DK Images; 6 ©Comstock Inc.; 8 (B) DK Images, (T) ©Comstock Inc.; 9 Getty Images; 10 ©Comstock Inc.; 12 DK Images; 13 DK Images; 14 (TL) DK Images, (BL) ©Comstock Inc.; 15 (TL, BR) ©Comstock Inc., (CL) DK Images

ISBN: 0-328-13314-0

A birthday is the day on which you were born. Everyone has a birthday. Many people around the world celebrate birthdays with special treats and activities. Children worldwide spend their special day in different ways.

Hi! I'm Aisha and I live in the United States. Today I am turning seven. My birthday is my favorite day of the year. My friends and family are coming to our house to celebrate with me. We are going to share a birthday cake with seven candles and play lots of games. My friends will bring me gifts. I'm going to have fun!

Dad will cook food on the grill outside. Mom and I will blow up lots of colorful balloons. We will play Pin the Tail on the Donkey. At the end of the day, I'll give each of my friends a bag with a surprise in it. It's a tiny bubble maker. Shhhh! Don't tell anyone!

Pin the Tail on the Donkey

Russia

Hi! I'm Ilya and I live in Russia. Yesterday was my seventh birthday. It was great! I woke up and found a present in a basket on the chair by my bed. My aunt had made a card for me. In Russia we eat a special birthday pie. My mom baked it and carefully wrote my name in the crust.

My family and friends came to my celebration. For fun we all wore hats and masks, and played a singing game called "The Round Loaf." My friends made a circle around me and let me have the first turn. I felt special all day. I can't wait to turn eight next year!

Party mask

Mexico

Hola! My name is Rosa and I live in Mexico. Today I am seven. This morning a mariachi band came to my home and sang a birthday song for me. It is called a *serenata*. The singers were my uncles and cousins. They woke me up! Then, my grandma invited everyone in for breakfast.

Piñata

Later, we had a big party with a *piñata*. A piñata is made of colorful paper. My piñata was filled with candy, nuts, and little toys. My dad hung the piñata in a tree, and we all took turns swinging the bat at it. It was hard because my mom tied a scarf over our eyes.

When the piñata burst, the goodies flew everywhere, and my friends and I scrambled to pick them up! My mom also made a cake called Three-Milk Cake. I made three wishes when I ate my piece, but I can't tell you what my birthday wishes are. If I do they might not come true!

My name is Yoshiko and I just turned seven today. Today has been a great day! Seven is an important age in Japan.

My mother made a special meal of beans and rice. She made a cake too. Lots of people came to see me and brought me presents. My aunt gave me a beautiful Japanese dress, called a *kimono*, to wear to special events.

At my party, all of us made birds. We folded them from special small, pretty, tissue paper. Making things from paper like this is called *origami*. I really like it. My friends gave me the birds they made. Birds mean good luck in Japan. I think my next year will be very lucky!

Paper origami birds

In this book you learned about how children in the United States, Russia, Mexico, the Philippines, and Japan celebrate birthdays. There are special treats, and the birthday boy or girl may get presents, sing songs, or play games.

Faces and Places
Around the World

AISHA, United States

ROSA, Mexico

Everywhere, people have different celebrations to honor their friends and relatives for different reasons. Do you celebrate your mom or dad on Mother's or Father's Day? What about Grandparent's Day? What are some other celebrations in your country? Shouldn't everyone get to feel special on their day?

ILYA, Russia

YOSHIKO, Japan

VICTOR, Philippines

15

Glossary

aunt *n.* your mother or father's sister, or your uncle's wife.

bank *n.* a place where people keep their money.

basket *n.* something to carry or store things in.

collect *v.* to gather or bring things together.

favorite *adj.* the thing you like better than all the others.

present *n.* a gift.